Nate & Shea's Adventures in IRELAND

By Carrie Whitten-Simmons
with help and journal entries from Nathan and Seamus, hosts of the television series *Travel With Kids*

Look for QR codes like this throughout the book. Scan with your smartphone or tablet to see video of Nate & Shea's travels in Ireland

(May require QR code reader app.)

Dedicated to Sally O'Malley, the best Irish mother and grandmother for which a person could hope. Your acceptance, humor, love and compassion has inspired many!

SPECIAL THANKS TO THE LORETO SISTERS OF SS. SIMON AND JUDE SCHOOL FOR SHARING YOUR IRISH CULTURE AND HISTORY WITH US

Fáilte! Pronounced fahl-che, means welcome in Irish Gaelic, a language still widely spoken in Ireland. The people of Ireland are proud of their rich history and culture and it shows in the music, dancing and *craic*, or fun, had all over the country. Join us, Nate and Shea, hosts of television series *Travel With Kids*, as we discover a thing or two about Ireland and stop for lots of fun along the way!

Located west of the island of Great Britain, Ireland is an island that hosts two countries: The Republic of Ireland and Northern Ireland. Known for its Irish dancing and music, rolling hills and sheep, lucky leprechauns and ancient legends, Irish culture is celebrated around the world, especially around St. Patrick's Day. Now a mostly peaceful and prosperous country, it wasn't always that way with tragic events like the Great Famine and the Troubles scarring its history.

Did you know...
- Over 3 million sheep live in Ireland
- Over 70 million people around the world claim Irish ancestry
- The original presidential White House and the Academy Awards' Oscar statue were designed by Irish people

In Ireland's flag:
Green = Irish people
Orange = English settlers in the north who supported William of Orange
White = Peace between the two groups

Ireland's coast has towering cliffs that give way to rolling green hills that are dotted by sheep. Check them out at the Cliffs of Moher and on the Dingle Peninsula where you can meet their famous resident Fungi the Dolphin!

NORTH CHANNEL

Donegal

Belfast

Ireland

Northern Ireland

IRISH SEA

Grace O'Malley Castle

Athlone

Galway

Dublin

Republic of Ireland

Wicklow

ARAN ISLANDS

The Burren

Cliffs of Moher

Limerick

DINGLE PENINSULA

Killarney

Tipperary

Waterford

Kenmare

Cork

Cliffs of Moher

Dingle Peninsula

Tombs found all over Ireland prove that humans have been living there for about 10,000 years. The most famous tomb is Newgrange (below left), which was built before the Egyptian pyramids. In the Burren, on Ireland's west coast, there are over 60 portal tombs, or dolmens, like the one pictured here (right). During the Neolithic era, people hunted and gathered food and used stone tools and later, began farming and forming communities. Some of these rock formations align with the sun during solstices, which may have helped predict growing seasons.

Poulnabroune Dolmen
The Burren

During the Iron Age, Celtic people began arriving in Ireland from mainland Europe. Ireland is one of the largest of the Celtic nations, or regions where Celtic culture has survived. The others are: Scotland, Wales, Brittany (in France), Cornwall (in Southwest England), and Isle of Man (in the Irish Sea). During this time clans ruled Ireland, with several strong clans forming kingdoms including Ulaid, Connacht, Munster and Leinster. There were wealthy clan leaders, warriors and scholars. Druids were also very important. They were sorcerers with supernatural powers who were often consulted to read signs and tell the future.

"An Arch Druid in his Judicial Habit"

Northern
Uí Néill

Ulaid

Bréifne

Airgíalla

Linns

Connacht
Connachta

Southern Uí Néill

Dublin

Leinster
Laign

Osraige

Limerick
Luimnech

Munster
mumu

Wexford

Waterford

Cork
Corcaigh

Irish Gaelic

Celtic people spoke Gaelic, a language that is still widely spoken in parts of Ireland today. Here are a few words to learn:

ENGLISH	IRISH GAELIC	PRONUNCIATION
HELLO	DIA DUIT	DEE-AH GWIT
BYE	SLAN AGAT	SHLAWN AH-GOOTH
PLEASE	LE DO THOIL	LEH DOO HULL
THANK YOU	GO RAIBH MAITH AGUTH	GO REV MA HA-GOOTH
EXCUSE ME	GABH MO LEITHSCEIL	GAH MOH LESH-SCALE
YES/NO	SEA/NI	SHAH/NEE
WHAT IS YOUR NAME?	CAD IS ANIM DUIT?	CAWD IS ANIM DIT?
HOW ARE YOU?	CONAS ATA TU?	COO-NAHS AHTAH TOO?
GOOD	GO MAITH	GO-MOH
CHEERS!	SLAINTE	SHLAHN-TEH
FUN	CRAIC	CRACK

IRISH GAELIC IS ONE OF THE OFFICIAL LANGUAGES OF IRELAND. LOOK FOR IT ON ROAD SIGNS.

Almost 100,000 people use Irish Gaelic daily (2011 Census)

6

Irish Mythology

The Tuatha Dé Danann, or "tribe of gods", were Irish gods with powers similar to gods in Roman mythology. They came to Ireland on clouds that covered the sun for three days. Their king, Nuada, led them to victory against the Fir Blog and Fomorians, two groups of semi-divine beings similar to the Greek Titans. The gods brought four magical items to Ireland: The Dagda's Cauldron, The Spear of Lugh, The Stone of Fal and The Sword of Light (pictured on stamp). Later, the Milesians arrived from what is now Spain. These were the Celtic people for which Ireland is so well known.

Ireland got its name from the goddess Éire.

One of the most popular characters in Irish legends was the great warrior hero Cú Chulainn, or "Culann's hound", in reference to a fierce beast he slayed when he was young. When he was on the battlefield, he turned into a monsterous rage...like the Tasmanian Devil. Below, he is pictured fighting the entire Connacht army by himself while the other warriors of Ulster were under a spell. Cú Chulainn and the giant hero to the south, Fionn mac Cumhaill, fought epic battles!

Sometimes I feel like going wild like the "Hound of Ulster"

Fionn mac Cumhaill was raised in the forest in secret to protect him. Some say he was a giant. As a boy, he burned himself while cooking the "salmon of knowledge" for a druid. He put his finger in his mouth to cool it and gained worldly wisdom. Later, he rescued the people of Tara from a fire-breathing fairy and became the leader of the Fianna people. Fionn and the Fianna people are said to sleep in a cave below Ireland to defend the island.

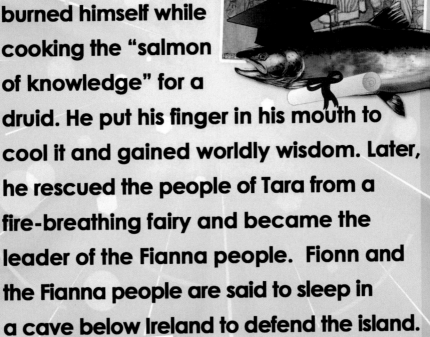

Of Man or Nature?

The strange rock formations of Giant's Causeway in Northern Ireland have baffled visitors for centuries. According to legend, Fionn created the stone bridge as a path to Scotland to battle his rival. Although the stones look manmade most scientists today say they are the result of volcanic activity.

Giant's Causeway

Irish Legends

Ireland is filled with mythical creatures and legends. In one story, King Lir's wife turns his childen into swans. In another, a harp puts a warring tribe to sleep.

The shamrock has had special meaning throughout time. The druids throught it had special powers because of the three heart shapes. Christians believe it represents the Holy Trinity: God the Father, the Son and the Holy Spirit.

The Claddagh symbolizes love (heart), friendship (hands) and loyalty (crown). It is commonly made into a ring, often used as a wedding ring.

Leprechauns

Leprechauns and fairies are a part of many Irish stories. Leprechauns are solitary creatures that live in caves or holes in the ground. They are known for causing lots of mischief and being able to talk themselves out of trouble! Many people associate them with pots of gold, which they guard at the end of rainbows! If they are caught, a leprechaun must grant three wishes. Legends of leprechauns date back to the 8th century.

Nathan's Journal

Date: / /   Subject: _____

We looked for Leprechan over the rainbow but we did not find any.

Christianity

Christianity arrived in Ireland in about the 5th century. You can see where monks lived in remote places like Skellig Michael to focus on God. It was in a monastery like this that the Book of Kells was created. Today, more than 80% of the people in the Republic of Ireland are Catholic. Much of the art of Ireland is centered around religious symbols like the high crosses pictured here.

The Book of Kells is an illuminated manuscript from the 9th century. Its ornate pictures tell the stories of the prophets of the Bible's New Testament. It can be viewed at Trinity College in Dublin.

12

St. Patrick

A representative of all things Ireland, St. Patrick was actually born in Scotland. As a young boy, he was captured by pirates and worked as a slave in Ireland. When he was 20 years-old, God came to him in a dream and told him to go to the ocean to escape. He found a boat to take him back to his family. In a later dream, he heard the people of Ireland calling for him to come back. After he became a bishop, he went to Ireland and converted many people to Christianity using the shamrock to explain the Trinity of God: the Father, Jesus and the Holy Spirit.

Seamus' Journal

Date: / /   Subject: _____

In Ireland they wear living shamrocks on their jackets on stpatricks day.

St. Brigid

Brigid of Ireland has a close connection to St. Patrick. He baptised her mother who was a slave. According to legend, Brigid performed many miracles, even in childhood. One story says Brigid gave all her family's butter to a needy family. And then, it reappeared in answer to her prayers. In the 5th century, Brigid founded a center for religious learning in Kildare. She also started a school of art, which created the Book of Kildare, a religious book similar to the Book of Kells.

Brigid's Cross first made by her for a dying man to explain cross and Christianity

"There was so great a friend-ship of charity that they had but one heart and one mind."
- *Book of Armagh on St. Patrick and St. Brigid*

St. Brendan the Navigator

Feast Day: May 16

Born in the 400s, Brendan is known for his journey to the "Isle of the Blessed". Studying at Clonard Abbey under St.Finnian, he is one of the "Twelve Apostles of Ireland". He became a priest in 512AD and sailed to islands like the Aran Islands on Ireland's west coast and as far as France spreading God's word. In his most famous journey, he set sail on the Atlantic Ocean with fourteen monks seeking the Garden of Eden. During this trip, he is said to have landed on a sea monster mistaking it for an island.

Some say the island he found was North America, which would make him first European to see it

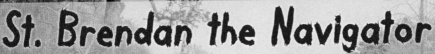

Middle Ages

In about 800AD, Vikings arrived in Ireland. They raided monasteries and established trading posts that are the base of Ireland's biggest cities, like Dublin and Cork. During the Middle Ages, castles were built to house wealthy landowners, knights and scholars. In nearby towns, common people raised livestock like pigs and sheep and farmed. One of the most famous castles is Bunratty Castle near Ennis. In the 1200s the Normans arrrived followed by the English who wanted to make sure they stayed in power.

Bunratty Castle has farm animals & shops around the castle...and you can go to banquet and eat with your hands like in Middle Ages!

Medieval Banquet

During the Middle Ages, the wealthy land-owners and knights had huge banquets with lots of food, music and dancing. Have an Ireland night: dress up like ladies and lords, put some harp music on and make turkey legs or the following recipe.

Corned Beef and Vegetables:

Place corned beef roast in roasting pan. Surround with 25 baby carrots, six potatoes, and one onion. (veggies should be cut into bite size pieces). Pour 1/2 a Guinness beer over top of the meat and sprinkle with 1/4 cup of brown sugar. Add enough water to cover vegetables. Cook at 300 degrees for about 5 hours. In last 1/2 hour add cabbage.

To make it an authentic Medieval meal, eat with your hands!

Corned beef and cabbage is not typically served in Ireland, but is considered an Irish dish

Dublin

In the 10th century, Vikings established a settlement near the River Liffey called "Dyflinn", a version of the Gaelic name of "Duibhlinn" meaning Black Pool. After Normans invaded, the city became a strong hold for the leader Strong-bow and was a center of trade. In the 12th century, King Henry II of England declared himself Lord of Ireland. In 1204, he had Dublin Castle built. The castle was used to house people in power, as a treasury, and as a prison. Dublin became the English power base in Ireland and they built sites like Trinity College. Today over one million people live in the Dublin area and it has lots of cool parks like St. Stephen's Green.

Brian Boru

During the 11th century, Brian Boru rose to power and united Ireland. He was born in the 900s as one of twelve sons of the king of what is now County Clare. Later, he became

King of Munster. After many huge battles, Boru became High King of Ireland ending domination by Ulster. The rulers of Leinster and Ulster were not happy. They banned together to fight Boru along with a force of Vikings. And, at the Battle of Clontarf in 1014, Boru was killed.

Battle of Clontarf by Hugh Frazer, 182

Boru used River Shannon and coasts for surprise attacks

The English Land

After years of fighting amongst the Irish and Norman clans and revolutions launched on the island, the English decided the island should be under their rule. As part of their conquest of Ireland, they confiscated Irish-owned land and put in place harsh laws against non-Protestants including banning Catholics from running for office and banishing clergymen. Tensions rose and the country entered into a long and brutal series of wars.

Known as "Old Ironsides" Oliver Cromwell was a member of the English Parliament and commander of the English conquest of Ireland. In Ireland, he is known for the brutality he showed to the Irish people. Later, he was Lord Protectorate of England, Scotland, Wales and Ireland.

Orange and the Green

With British rule came fighting between English Protestant and Irish Catholic people, which is reflected in Irish songs and dances like the Orange and the Green. Why those colors? The orange represents loyalty to William of Orange, Protestant king of England who fought the overthrown Catholic king of England, James II, in the Battle of the Boyne in 1690 in Ireland. The green represents the native Irish Catholics. William of Orange won which led to continued Protestant domination and more fighting.

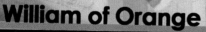

James II

William of Orange

Blarney Castle

Although there has been a castle here since the 1200s, the current castle was built by Cormac MacCarthy in 1446. It was taken by English forces in the Williamite wars. Today, many tourists visit Blarney Castle to kiss the Blarney Stone. According to legend, he who kisses the stone will be blessed with the gift of gab, or be able to sweet talk their way out of anything. Many people say this started when MacCarthy convinced Queen Elizabeth I to let him keep the rights to his land after kissing the stone.

To kiss Blarney Stone hang upside down in here

Nathan's Journal

Date : / /   Subject : _____

It was scary turning upside down so high up in the air but it was still a great experience!

Family Crest

Each clan in Ireland had a different family crest. Most crests were shield shaped and had figures to represent their family. These crests were often painted on shields and flags and carried into battle.

The crest typically included a motto and graphics.
Make your own shield:
- 1/2" foam board
- 2 - 12" elastic straps
- Paint
- Stapler/staples

Draw a shield shape on foam board. Cut it out. Pick two colors, one lighter and one darker works best. Decide on a design (ideas below). Sketch it on shield. Paint it. If you would like, add an animal like a lion, bear, eagle, boar, horse or dragon...anything you feel represents you. Staple top of elastic straps 5" from the top/5" from each side of shield. Stretch them to 5" from bottom (or as far as they will reach) and staple the bottoms. This is the slot for your arm. And you are ready to go!

Paint your colors and...

...ta-da, a crest for your shield!

Grace O'Malley

Many Irish families living in other countries can trace their ancestory to a particular clan in Ireland. One of the largest clans in County Mayo was the O'Malley clan; most famous for one of their leaders, the first female pirate: Grace O'Malley. When she was young, Grace wanted to work on her father's ships. They traded goods far away. He told her that ships were no place for a girl. So, according to legend, she cut her hair and went aboard. Over time, she gained respect amongst the men of the clan and   was put in charge of the shipping fleet. She married the head of the O'Flaherty clan and had three kids: Owen, Margaret and Murrough.

I'm related to a pirate! Grace O'Malley is a long lost relative!

The Pirate Queen

After her first husband died, she married Richard Bourke and had a son, Theobald. After one year, she divorced him by locking herself in Rockfleet Castle and yelling down at him, "I dismiss you." It was his castle. She kept it. The English Council was getting complaints that her ships were acting like pirates; boarding other ships and charging a "toll" of cash or cargo, which gave her the nickname "Pirate Queen". When her sons were captured by the English, she sailed to England and met with Queen Elizabeth I (pictured). They came to an agreement, which freed her sons, but they both broke it soon afterwards.

Seamus' Journal
Subject :
Date   /   /
It was amazing exploring grace O'malleys Castle, that would be cool to live in one!

Emigration

Many people in the world can trace their heritage to Ireland because throughout the years, Ireland has had

Emigrants Leave Ireland by Henry O'Doyle

a lot of people leave. During the English rule, many left in hopes of a better life or were sent as slaves or indentured servants to work in English colonies. But, the biggest exodus of people was during the Great Famine or Potato Famine from 1845 to 1852. During this time about one million people left Ireland. Those that stayed were starving as the potato was the main food source for poor people. Today, more than 80 million people around the world can trace at least some of their ancestors to Ireland.

Irish Culture on the Rise

Under English rule, Irish langauge and traditions had been oppressed, but as Irish nationalism and independence movements grew, so did pride in Irish Gaelic culture. Today, Irish music is famous around the world with bands like U2, Van Morrison, The Pogues, The Cranberries and The Dubliners and songs like *Danny Boy* and *When Irish Eyes Are Smiling* being pub sing-along favorites throughout the world. Irish dance is globally performed with Michael Flatley's *Riverdance* drawing huge audiences.

Gaelic sports like hurling host huge competitions around the world too.

When Irish Eyes Are Smiling has been recorded by over 200 artists

Irish Music

Spontaneous Irish music sessions happen quite often in pubs with musicians gathering to play traditional instruments. Other people clap along and often break into song or tell stories or poems. Some instruments you might see include: Celtic harp, bodhrán drum, fiddle, accordion, Irish flute and more. The harp is a symbol of Ireland. Bagpipes are also a traditional Irish instrument, but usually they are played outdoors.

Nathan's Journal

Subject :

Date   /   /

It was fun to dance
in the irish pubs. I
even got to play the
drums!

Irish dance

Irish dance has become popular for kids to learn around the world. Perhaps the most famous Irish dancers are from *Riverdance*. Here are a few steps you can learn at home.

Jump Step:

Start position: Stand tall, arms at side with right foot forward, toe pointed.

Step 1: Hop forward on right foot, kicking left foot up to your bottom.

Step 2: Swing left foot forward and step on it wth it in a turned out position.

Step 3: Pick up right foot and move it so that toe touches heel of left foot.

(Right foot should now be behind left foot facing forward and left foot in front and turned out at a 90 degree angle)

When you have this down, start the step again with the other foot. Link several Jump Steps together while moving in a circle to make a dance. Try holding a partners hand while doing the Jump Step too.

TIP: Arms always stay tight, straight down at your sides or on your hips!

Gaelic Sports

Many members of the early Gaelic Athletic Association were also part of the independence movement and along with the Irish culture, Gaelic sports have been on the rise. Here are a few to try.

Gaelic football: Played between two teams of 15 players. A ball is kicked, thrown, bounced and passed to a goal post where it can be thrown over or under for various points.

Hurling: Thousands of years old, hurling is played between two teams of 15 players. It is like a cross between lacrosse and baseball. It moves very fast as teams try to hit a ball above or below a bar/goal at the end of the field.

Gaelic Handball: Similar to raquetball, but played by hitting a ball against a wall with the hand to prevent your opponent from returning it.

Rounders: A bat and ball game similar to baseball.

Rounders game, 1913

Sinn Féin & the IRA

Founded in 1905, Sinn Féin means "we our-selves". It is a political group that played a key role in getting independence for Ireland. In 1917, Sinn Féin's main goal was to establish an Irish Republic. Leaders of the party worked with the Irish Volunteers, which would become the Irish Republican Army (IRA), to stage the Easter Rising. While Sinn Féin was the political voice for independence, the IRA headed the armed struggle. In 1918, the party won about 3/4 of the seats in Parliament and in 1919 declared them-selves Dáil Éireann, or the Parliament of Ireland.

In early 2000s, Sinn Féin worked with Northern Ireland Unionist parties to establish peace through a new power-sharing government

Easter Rising

During Easter Week 1916, Irish republicans rose up against the British. Patrick Pearse and James Connolly, led over 1,000 members of the Irish Volunteers and Irish Citizen Army, to seize key locations in Dublin and proclaim a new, independent government. Though Irish forces surrendered in less than a week, many people were killed or wounded. The British arrested over 3,000 Sinn Féin members. Many leaders were executed at Kilmainham Gaol (jail). This increased support for Irish independence and membership in Sinn Féin.

Sinn Féin Parliament members declared independence for Ireland in 1919

POBLACHT NA H EIREANN.
THE PROVISIONAL GOVERNMENT
OF THE
IRISH REPUBLIC
TO THE PEOPLE OF IRELAND.

IRISHMEN AND IRISHWOMEN In the name of God and of the dead generations from which she receives her old tradition of nationhood, Ireland, through us, summons her children to her flag and strikes for her freedom.

Having organised and trained her manhood through her secret revolutionary organisation, the Irish Republican Brotherhood, and through her open military organisations, the Irish Volunteers and the Irish Citizen Army, having patiently perfected her discipline, having resolutely waited for the right moment to reveal itself, she now seizes that moment, and, supported by her exiled children in America and by gallant allies in Europe, but relying in the first on her own strength, she strikes in full confidence of victory.

We declare the right of the people of Ireland to the ownership of Ireland, and to the unfettered control of Irish destinies, to be sovereign and indefeasible. The long usurpation of that right by a foreign people and government has not extinguished the right, nor can it ever be extinguished except by the destruction of the Irish people. In every generation the Irish people have asserted their right to national freedom and sovereignty, six times during the past three hundred years they have asserted it in arms. Standing on that fundamental right and again asserting it in arms in the face of the world, we hereby proclaim the Irish Republic as a Sovereign Independent State, and we pledge our lives and the lives of our comrades-in-arms to the cause of its freedom, of its welfare, and of its exaltation among the nations.

The Irish Republic is entitled to, and hereby claims, the allegiance of every Irishman and Irishwoman. The Republic guarantees religious and civil liberty, equal rights and equal opportunities to all its citizens, and declares its resolve to pursue the happiness and prosperity of the whole nation and of all its parts, cherishing all the children of the nation equally, and oblivious of the differences carefully fostered by an alien government, which have divided a minority from the majority in the past.

Until our arms have brought the opportune moment for the establishment of a permanent National Government, representative of the whole people of Ireland and elected by the suffrages of all her men and women, the Provisional Government, hereby constituted, will administer the civil and military affairs of the Republic in trust for the people.

We place the cause of the Irish Republic under the protection of the Most High God, Whose blessing we invoke upon our arms, and we pray that no one who serves that cause will dishonour it by cowardice, inhumanity, or rapine. In this supreme hour the Irish nation must, by its valour and discipline and by the readiness of its children to sacrifice themselves for the common good, prove itself worthy of the august destiny to which it is called.

Signed on Behalf of the Provisional Government,
THOMAS J. CLARKE,
SEAN Mac DIARMADA,   THOMAS MacDONAGH,
P. H. PEARSE,   EAMONN CEANNT,
JAMES CONNOLLY.   JOSEPH PLUNKETT.

Ireland at War

After Sinn Féin published the Declaration of Independence, Ireland was at war. The Irish Republican Army fought British security forces including the Black and Tans in the War of Independence. Much of the violence took place in Dublin and Belfast, where many civilians were killed. On December 6, 1921, the Anglo-Irish treaty was signed creating an Irish Free State, which included the 26 counties of the Republic of Ireland, but not the six counties of Northern Ireland. Many Irish nationalists were against the treaty and so the fighting continued as the Irish Civil War.

Éamon de Valera

Born to an Irish mother in New York City in 1882, de Valera came to Ireland when he was two years-old. He was a Gaelic speaker, rugby player and promoter of Irish culture. In 1913, he joined the Irish Volunteers and was an Easter Rising commander. Unlike other rebel leaders, who were sentenced to death, de Valera got life in prison because of his U.S. birth. He was released in 1917 and elected president of Sinn Féin. In 1919, he visited the U.S. and raised millions of dollars for the independence movement. While he was gone, he left the government in the hands of Michael Collins. Unhappy with Collins' signing of the Anglo-Irish Treaty, de Valera headed the anti-Treaty IRA. In 1926, he formed a new party, Fianna Fáil. They won the most seats in the 1932 elections, which made de Valera the Prime Minister.

"It is indeed hard for the strong to be just to the weak, but acting justly always has its rewards."

Michael Collins

Born in 1890 in County Cork, Michael Collins grew up on a farm. Even from a young age his family knew he was meant for greatness. When he was 19, he joined the Irish Republican Brotherhood. After the Easter Rising, Collins, and thousands of other rebellion leaders, were sent to a prison in Wales. There, they discussed plans to continue the rebellion. By 1917, Collins was director of the Irish Volunteers and managed the IRA. The next year, he was elected as Sinn Féin representative from County Cork and joined in declaring Ireland independent. Collins was sent to negotiate peace during the War of Independence. He signed the Anglo-Irish treaty to which many people were opposed and which led to the Irish Civil War and his assassination in 1922.

"Give us the future, we've had enough of your past...give us back our country to live in, to grow in, to love."

The Troubles

The Anglo-Irish treaty left the six counties of Northern Ireland out of the new found Irish Free State, which increased tensions there. Generally, the Protestant English wanted to remain a part of the United Kingdom while the Irish Catholics wanted to unite with the south. The Irish Republican Army (IRA) was committed to uniting the two areas into one Irish nation. In the 1960s discrimination against Catholics and police brutality sparked the beginning of "The Troubles". The IRA began an armed struggle and established a "Free Derry" - a "no-go" zone for British forces. In 1972,British forces fired on unarmed protestors killing14 people and wounding many more; a day known as "Bloody Sunday".

U2 sings about events of Jan. 30, 1972 in song "Sunday Bloody Sunday"

Peace Agreement

As violence peaked, peace walls were put up to separate Catholic nationalist and Protestant unionist neighborhoods. In the 1980s, while the IRA increased violence, bombing targets outside of Northern Ireland, Sinn Féin, led by Gerry Adams, looked for a political solution to the problem. In 1998, the Good Friday Agreement, which proposed a power-sharing government, was signed. On May 8, 2007, members of opposing parties took office together. Today, the walls and murals serve as a reminder and as tourist attractions.

New government at Stormont
May 8, 2007

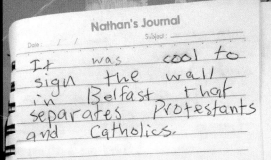

Nathan's Journal

Date: / /   Subject:

It was cool to sign the wall in Belfast that separates Protestants and Catholics.

Nate & Shea's Adventures provides information about destinations around the world. Learn history, culture and nature by taking a virtual trip with your guides Nate and Shea. *Nate & Shea's Adventures* can be used as a companion guide to the *Travel With Kids* video series or on their own.

Look for these other *Travel With Kids* products:

Nate & Shea's Adventures in:
Hawaii, South Africa, New York, Alaska Peru, London, Ireland, Wales, Italy, Florida

Travel With Kids (DVD):

United States:
Alaska
Florida
Hawaii: Oahu
Hawaii: Kaua'i
Hawaii: Maui & Moloka'i
Hawaii: Big Island
New York
San Diego

Caribbean:
Bahamas
Caribbean Cruise
Jamaica
Puerto Rico & Virgin Islands

Europe:
England
Greece
Ireland
Italy
London
Paris
Scotland
Wales

Latin America:
Costa Rica
Mexico: Yucatan
Mexico: Baja
Peru

Episodes covering additional destinations available on Hulu, iTunes, Amazon and more

Find out more at TravelWithKids.tv!

DREAMING OF THE FAMILY ADVENTURE OF A LIFETIME?

Now you can join us on a TWK Family AdventureTour from the creators of the TV series *Travel With Kids*

Volunteer   Reconnect time   Family time   Kid time   Adventure

FAMILY ADVENTURE TOURS 2016
THAILAND   SOUTH AFRICA   IRELAND

Customize Your Trip:

All TWK Family Adventure itineraries can be customized to fit your interests and dates

2016 Escorted Tours:

Thailand: Jungles & Beaches
June 18 - 28 and July 1 - 15

South Africa: Soweto & Safari
July 16 - 22

Ireland: Castles & Coasts
July 27 - August 5

Mexico: Mayan Riviera
October 8 - 15

Costa Rica: Jungles & Beaches
December 16 - 23 and Dec 26- Jan 2

TWK Family Adventure Destinations:

Mexico **Peru**
Fiji Costa Rica
Italy
South Africa
Ireland **Kenya**
Belize **Thailand**
and more...

Why TWK Family Adventure Travel & Tours?

- Pre-screened family-friendly itineraries
- Decades of family travel experience
- Turn key family vacations:
    You pick the destination, we do the work!
- Perfect mix of family time and separate time

www.TravelWithKids.tv

Made in the USA
Middletown, DE
14 March 2020